DAILY RITUALS

THE
DREAM
LIFE
PROJECT

Copyright © 2024 Cecilia Huang
First published 2024
The Dream Life Project
https://thedreamlifeproject.co
ISBN: 978-1-7638175-0-0

All rights reserved. No parts of the publication may be reproduced, distributed, or transmitted in any form or by any means including photocopying, recording, or other electronic or mechanical methods without prior written permission from the publisher.

Design and layout by Cecilia Huang

101 small acts to unlock happiness

DAILY RITUALS

CECILIA HUANG

introduction

Happiness is a gentle whisper, often just out of reach, especially in a world that seems to demand it at every turn, happiness can feel like a distant dream, always slipping through your fingers. But what if happiness isn't something to be chased, but rather something to be quietly welcomed into your life through small, tender acts?

In this book, we explore the idea that happiness doesn't have to be a grand, elusive prize. Instead, it's found in the quiet moments, the gentle rituals that bring you back to yourself and connect you to the world around you. This book invites you to redefine happiness, not as a destination, but as a series of small, mindful steps that you take every day.

Take a moment to consider what happiness truly means to you. It might be the peace of a morning spent in stillness, the warmth of a loved one's embrace, or the simple joy of giving to others.

Happiness grows when you share yourself with those you love and when you nurture deep, meaningful relationships that ground you and bring you joy.

By embracing the present moment, by being here, fully, in the now, you unlock the door to happiness. It's in these moments of connection and reflection that you find the true essence of a joyful life.

This book is a companion, guiding you through 101 small acts—each a gentle ritual designed to help you unlock happiness, day by day. Whether it's through a quiet morning reflection, a heartfelt conversation, or a moment of stillness before sleep, these rituals are the key to opening your heart to the happiness that is already within you.

Happiness isn't something to achieve; it's something to experience, here and now, in the rhythm of your daily life. Let this book be your guide as you embark on a journey of self-discovery, healing, and quiet joy, one small act at a time.

Cecilia

It isn't what you have, or who you are, or where you are, or what you are doing that makes you happy or unhappy, it is what you think about.

DALE CARNEGIE

1

focus on living

Happiness is not something to be pursued as an end in itself, but rather a natural by-product of living a meaningful life. It arises from when you are living in alignment with your values and purpose.

2

find your reason

Take time to reflect and work out your values and goals, to put it simply, what's important to you. It might be family, health, fitness, or community. Whatever it is, it's that which makes you get up and carry on day after day, and from it, your routines and actions will flow.

3

pursue your goals

The journey of pursuing something can bring you happiness, not just the end goal. When you immerse in activities that you are passionate about and that challenge you, you find meaning in the pursuit. Focus on the process, not just the outcome, and enjoy the challenges that come along the way.

4

define your success

You are the one to create your own benchmark and hold the measuring stick. What is really true for you? What falls within your control? What could happen if you define what success look like?

Success is peace of mind that is the direct result of self-satisfaction in knowing you did your best to become the best that you are capable of becoming.

JOHN WOODEN

5

follow your dreams

Regardless of your age or circumstances, the potential to become who you have always aspired to be remains within your grasp. It is never too late to pursue your passions and to actualise your true potential. Every day offers a fresh opportunity to follow your dreams.

6

live a big life

Pursue your wildest dreams. It can be scary to take that leap of faith, but the rewards are immeasurable. Don't let fear hold you back from living the life you're meant to live.

7

trust the universe

The universe has a plan for you that is even better than what you had imagined. Don't get caught up in your expectations that you forget to appreciate the unexpected beauty. Let go of control and allow life to unfold as it will.

8

enjoy the beauty of becoming

Waiting can be a blessing in disguise. It gives you time to reflect, grow, and prepare for what is to come. Trust the wait, it can lead you to unexpected opportunities. When nothing is certain, anything is possible.

9

define happy

Happy is a state of joy and contentment that you share with the world through your actions and kindness, as much as you experience it from the positive energies you receive from others.

Happy (adj):
'Feeling or showing pleasure or contentment.'

10

choose to be happy

Happiness isn't something that simply arrives, it is found in the small decisions you make each day to cultivate a positive mindset and enjoy the present moment. Choose to be happy every day.

11

don't self-sabotage

Self-sabotaging prevents you from living a life that you truly value. It keeps you trapped in your comfort zone. Don't let self-sabotaging disrupts your progress toward achieving your goals, hopes and dreams.

12

trust in yourself and your actions

Happiness is not something that can be forced or chased. Sometimes, it comes unexpectedly. Happiness isn't always about what you do, but about being open to the possibilities that life presents you with.

13

witness your growth

Happiness is not about specific virtues or pleasures, it's about the progress you make. Witnessing your growth brings you a sense of achievement, purpose, and fulfilment. You are genuinely happy as you evolve.

14

create your morning routine

Light a candle, say a mantra, listen to music, stretch or walk, write in your journal, or meditate. Bring mindfulness to your morning. Choose what works for you, and what is most nourishing for your mind and body. This is your morning and your creation.

15

take five deep breaths

The moment you wake up is a powerful transition from rest to wakefulness, and how you start your day can shape its entire flow. Before you get out of bed, bring your attention to your breath. Observe five mindful breaths, focusing your attention on the inhale and the exhale.

16

wrap yourself up

It can be hard to get up in the cold and dark, so make it a pleasure by keeping a cosy dressing gown and slippers beside your bed to snuggle into in the morning. Invest in something you really like to turn your first moments of the day into a cozy ritual.

17

start work with ease

Practise a 10-minute meditation at your desk before you start to work. Allow yourself this time before the busyness begins. Close your eyes and sit comfortably but upright with attention to your posture. Focus on your breath and witness its flow.

18

embrace work

Be passionate about what you are working on. Create something meaningful to bring you great joy and satisfaction. You have the power to illuminate the world around you. Find happiness in your work and the meaning you deliver.

19

pick a mindful daily activity

Choose one activity to do with mindfulness and observe each element of the activity. Whether it's feeling the warmth of the water in the shower, the texture of the soap lathering on your skin, or the gentle motion of your hands as you iron a shirt, bringing your attention to these small details creates a sense of connection to the now.

20

brush your teeth mindfully

Hold the toothbrush gently. Consider and apply the toothpaste to the toothbrush. Begin to brush deliberately and slowly. Breathe in and out through your nose. Relax your jaw. Feel the brush on your gums. Feel the sensation of clean teeth and give thanks for your teeth that help you to eat, smile and speak at will.

21

listen to your body

Lie down and close your eyes. Start at the top of your head or tip of your toes and mindfully scan your body. Stop at any points that require your attention and stay there until your mind drifts. Move between observation of detailed areas and whole body sensations. Allow as much, or as little time as you want.

22

check in with yourself

Despite the demands of kids, jobs, friends, and family, make time for yourself. Make it a habit to check in with yourself every day. Ask yourself how you are feeling today and whatever the answer is, try to accept it and honour it.

23

take a mindfulness minute

Set your timer to go off hourly as a reminder and choose a routine that works for you. It could be a stretch, a short walk or five deep breaths. Pay attention for one full minute then resume working. It's particularly beneficial to do this in the afternoon when concentration waves.

24

smile in the mirror

Your smile is like a boomerang, bouncing happiness back and forth between you and the world around you. Even if you're feeling a bit down, just putting on a smile can kickstart a chain reaction of happiness, turning your day around.

Sometimes your joy is the source of your smile, but sometimes your smile can be the source of your joy.

THÍCH NHẤT HẠNH

25

drink a glass of water mindfully

Water quenches your thirst and helps you reconnect with the natural rhythm of your body. It purifies your body, flushing out toxins, and helps release the stresses of the day. Drink it slowly, breathe between sips, then wash and dry the glass ready for next time.

26

finish your work mindfully

Just as at the beginning of your day, take time to prepare for the next phase. Turn off the phone and laptop and just be. Focus on your breath and let your thoughts come and go like clouds in the sky, clearing the path to joyful communication with those you love at home.

27

go for a walk

As your feet move, so do your minds, often leading to bursts of creativity and clarity. Whether it's a leisurely stroll in nature or a brisk walk through your neighbourhood, walking can stimulate great ideas and reflections.

All truly great thoughts are conceived while walking.

NIETZSCHE

28

think before buying

Before you hand over your credit card or hit send at the online checkout, pause for a moment and ask yourself why you are making this purchase. Do you really need it or are you fulfilling an urge? Will it burden you with clutter and financial stress or improve your life? Walk away if you need to.

29

want less

Limiting your desires can lead to greater happiness. By simplifying your life, you can focus on the things that truly matter. Let go of the desire for material possessions and make room for the experiences that truly bring you joy.

30

create positive routines

Happiness is not something that is achieved once and for all, but rather a daily practice of simple disciplines. Your daily choices have a significant impact on your overall level of happiness. Strive to cultivate positive habits.

31

respect your mind

Happiness lies in your mind. It is your internal perspective and the way you choose to perceive and think about your circumstances that ultimately determine your level of happiness. Focus on the good in your life, even in challenging times.

32

remember good times

Instead of being bummed out that it's over, appreciate the fact that it happened. Those moments, whether big or small, shaped you and added to your story. Be grateful for the wonderful experiences you've had and smile because they became part of your memory.

33

be the sunshine

When you can't find the sunshine, be the sunshine. You have the innate power to create your own happiness. Be your own sunshine and be a source of light for others, spreading joy and kindness wherever you go.

34

think positive

Your thoughts create your world. If you choose to think positively, you will create a world filled with love and abundance. You will begin to see the beauty and wonder in the world around you.

35

keep striving

Happy people are constantly striving for something better. The absence of certain things you desire is a necessary component of happiness. Your happiness not solely depends on what you have, but also what you can do without.

36

let happiness flow

True moments of happiness take you by surprise. These moments can be incredibly powerful. It is not that you seize them, but that they seize you. Be open to and appreciate the small moments of happiness that come by surprise.

37

notice the little things

Being present and mindful is the key to enjoying happiness. You miss out on happiness not because you never found it, but because you were too busy to truly appreciate it. Be present, be mindful, notice and enjoy the little things.

38

don't overthink it

People who are searching the hardest to be happy are often the unhappiest. Next time you find yourself pining for happiness, try shifting your attention towards activities and relationships that bring you joy.

39

consider your purpose

To make the most of exercise and remain committed to it, it helps to understand your motivation for doing it. It could be to lose weight, have more energy, and help cope with the pressure of work and life. Write down your purpose and place it somewhere handy so you can check in with it before you start.

40

seize the moment

Happiness is not something that is given to you, but rather something that you actively pursue and create for yourself. Seize happiness whenever you can, and don't waste a minute not being happy.

41

don't take it for granted

Happiness is a fleeting and ephemeral experience. Like a cloud, it drifts through your life, beautiful yet ever-changing. If you try to hold onto it for too long, it slips away. Savour happiness in the moment, rather than fixating on it.

42

keep it simple

Happiness is health and a short memory. Eat healthily, drink plenty of water, exercise daily and sleep well. Choose to see things on the bright side, and not allow past experiences to define your present and future happiness.

43

treat each day as special

Happiness is about approaching each day with a sense of wonder and joy. Live every single day with the excitement of the first day of your honeymoon and the bittersweet of the last day of your vacation.

44

be like a kid

Happiness is always within reach. No one can stay gloomy when holding a balloon. It's simple, colourful, and brings an instant smile to your face.

45

practise acceptance

The more you accept things as they are, the happier you become. Acceptance doesn't mean giving up on dreams or ambitions, it's about finding contentment in what you have now.

trust your desire to be happy

Happiness isn't just a destination or a fleeting moment, it's something you can enjoy fully when you stop, appreciate it, and be present with it, rather than constantly pursuing the next thrill.

47

don't sweat the small stuff

Your happiness often lies in your own hands. The little frustrations that pop up can seem huge at the moment, but by deciding not to let the small stuff upset you, you create space for more peace. You hold the power of how you react to things. Don't let little things steal your peace.

48

know your sweet spot

When you let go of constant self-concern and immerse yourself in the little joys of daily life, happiness naturally follows. Your ordinary days hold the potential for extraordinary contentment.

49

make a plan

Focus on the actions you can take to create a fulfilling life, rather than obsessing over the end result. Take control of your life and pursue your passions, rather than waiting for happiness to come to you.

50

have a purge

Through tidying, you confront your possessions and the emotional attachment. Through cleaning, you confront the messes and dirt that nature can leave behind. Approach cleaning as a way to connect with nature and take care of your environment.

51

tend to your plants

Planting and watching something grow offers a profound sense of peace in a world that often feels rushed. Find enduring happiness rooted in the cycles of nature and the care you put into nurturing life.

52

give your love

Love, in its purest form, brings out the best in you. When you give your time, energy, or resources, you not only uplift others but also enrich your own life. Happiness is found in the joy of making a positive impact on those around you.

53

look after others

True meaning in life often comes from the responsibilities you take on. Responsibility gives you purpose, driving you to grow, persevere, and contribute to something greater than yourself.

54

lift a friend up

When you brighten up a friend's day, you light up your own. True joy often comes from seeing the smiles and relief you bring to others. By giving support, you invite happiness into your own life.

The best way to cheer yourself is to try to cheer someone else up.

MARK TWAIN

55

care about community

You have the power to make a difference, whether it's within your own community, your nation, or the world. Your unique gifts and abilities can heal the brokenness and create a better world for everyone.

56

think of ways to give

You get more joy out of giving joy to others. Unlike buying for yourself, which delivers short-lived pleasure, gifting to another person continues to make you feel fresh, new and pleasurable.

57

make somebody's day

Your happiness is deeply intertwined with the joy you spread. It is a present reality that you can access right now. By making others happy, you create your own joy now and here.

The time to be happy is now. The place to be happy is here. The way to be happy is to make others so.

Robert Green Ingersoll

58

be a good company

Take your friend on a walk, enjoy a meal with them outdoors, or simply open up some windows in their home to let in lots of fresh air. Fresh air really does something that just helps brighten a dark day. It definitely helps.

59

value your neighbour

No matter how affluent you may be, the support, connection, and companionship of neighbours and friends are invaluable. Community provide a sense of belonging and enrich your life in ways that money cannot.

60

leave a note for a stranger

Simple, positive affirmations are powerful. You can bring a smile and spark a moment of connection with a stranger by saying something positive like "You've got this" or "Today is the day to be happy".

61

look out for yourself

When you treat yourself with compassion and care, you build the emotional resilience for spreading kindness. By taking care of your physical, mental, and emotional needs, you are better able to extend happiness to those around you.

62

accept mistakes

Failure is not the end but a step in the journey of improvement. Each attempt teaches you valuable lessons. By embracing failure as an opportunity to grow, you transform setbacks into stepping stones towards better outcomes.

63

high five yourself

The deepest happiness comes from knowing that you are loved unconditionally. You are not alone in the world. You are valued and cherished for who you are, with all your imperfections. You are loved and worthy of love, just as you are.

64

forgive others

Forgiveness is not about condoning wrongs but about freeing yourself from the burden of resentment. Forgive others so you can heal from pain and loss, reclaim your peace and open the door to happiness.

65

unstuck yourself

If something doesn't go your way, don't beat yourself up. Accept it as an hiccup on the way to achieving your goals. Thank it for what it teaches you. Get back to your focus with greater wisdom.

learn to let go of anger

Anger and happiness cannot exist in the same moment. When you hold onto anger, you lose precious time that could have been spent experiencing happiness. Learn to let go of anger and focus on the positive aspects of your life.

For every minute you are angry you lose sixty seconds of happiness.

RALPH WALDO EMERSON

67

say thank you

From the whispered kindness of a stranger to the grandeur of a starlit sky, every experience offers a reason to give thanks. Shift your focus from problems to blessings, and embrace all the moments that colour your life.

68

be your own cheerleader

Instead of being your toughest critic, be your own biggest cheerleader. Be on your own side, and believe in yourself unconditionally, that's the key to unlocking your true potential.

69

treat yourself

Go for a sunrise walk, curl up on the sofa with a good book, visit a day spa, or enjoy a solo dinner. Making time and doing something nice for yourself can give you a happiness boost.

70

look for laughter

Laughter lightens your mood and helps you navigate through challenges with a positive outlook and renewed strength. Have a little laughter. Look around you for happiness.

71

nurture your tribe

Happiness is cultivated in everyday interactions with your friends. Make new friends and expand your social circles. Value the friendships in your life and make an effort to maintain them.

72

value your network

By being kind to everyone, liking many, and loving a few deeply, you build meaningful relationships. These bonds form the foundation of your happiness and enrich your life in countless ways.

73

collaborate in a team

Working collectively provides opportunities to learn, connect with others' thoughts and ideas, and leverage talents and skills. A shared vision may also provide something to hope for, something to do and something to love.

74

recognise others

Think about the people who helped you become who you are today. Someone who took a chance on you early in your career, someone who encouraged you in a passion, someone who inspired you, believed in you or offered a shoulder when you needed one. Be grateful to all these people.

75

value your friends

As you journey through life, you'll meet different people and form connections that range from acquaintances to lifelong friends. While it's exciting to expand your social circles, cherish and value the old friends who have been with you through thick and thin.

Make new friends, but keep the old: those are silver, these are gold.

JOSEPH PARRY

76

keep making new friends

Step out of your comfort zone, continue to make new friends through work or volunteer; go for a walk in the park or to a local café and be open to new conversations. The ability to keep making new friends brings unlimited capacity for happiness.

77

have a good attitude

Like adding a dash of sunshine to your morning coffee, a good attitude makes everything a little brighter. When that positive vibe keeps on rolling, it turns a great day into a great month which becomes a great year and beyond.

78

pay a compliment

Be generous with compliments. It costs nothing, yet its value is immeasurable. You have the power to make someone's day with just a few words. Tell your friend her hair looks great, congratulate your colleague on the report they just presented, and tell a stranger on the street you love their dress.

79

give a hug

You need four hugs a day for survival, eight for maintaining your health, and twelve for growth. Embrace the power of these simple, warm touches, they are crucial to your emotional and physical wellbeing.

80

focus on today

Today is the perfect day to be happy. Yesterday is dead, tomorrow hasn't arrived yet. You have just one day, today, to be happy in it.

81

be satisfied

Shift your focus from what you lack to what you already have. Sometimes you get so caught up in chasing after what you don't have and forget to appreciate what you do have.

82

don't compare to others

The only comparison that matters is with yourself. Everyone's journey is different, you have unique gifts that others don't. Don't look to other people to measure your own performance.

Don't let your ice cream melt while you're counting somebody else's sprinkles.

AKILAH HUGHES

83

let it go

Holding on to past grievances, regrets, or unmet expectations can weigh you down. By releasing what no longer serves you, you create space for new experiences. That is the key to happiness.

84

journal daily

Unleash your superpower for self-reflection and creativity with journalling. Writing daily is a great way to manage ideas and self-healing, and to uncover patterns in your thoughts and moods.

85

move your body

When it comes to working out, there's no such thing as a bad session. Even if you're not feeling the burn or hitting personal records, just showing up and getting it done is a win.

86

see a sunset

Add a sunset to the end of your day, and remind yourself no matter what happens, every day can end beautifully. Nature is nourishing; getting outside helps you reset and centre, feeling deeply grateful for the natural world.

87

create space

Create space to flourish by weeding out what doesn't serve you. Cultivate your inner happiness by exploring your subconscious, and take some quiet time to let your 'thought seeds' take root and transform into wildflowers.

88

declutter

Just because it doesn't spark joy for you right now doesn't mean it's worthless. Items that no longer serve you can bring joy and utility to others. Declutter what you no longer need, and embrace a cycle of giving and receiving. Remember that value is subjective and ever-changing.

89

find your inner child

Children have a way of seeing the world with fresh eyes. Tap into your inner child and see the world as if for the first time. Rediscover the magic in even the most ordinary things. Just as children joyfully splash in puddles during a downpour, you too can find delight amidst life's rainy days.

90

let love in

Practising gratitude helps you see the world in a whole new light. When you start counting your blessings, the things you've been chasing don't seem as important anymore. It's like realising you've been standing in a field of wildflowers all along, too busy looking elsewhere to notice.

91

acknowledge milestones

Bring your loved ones together to celebrate your next milestone. Weddings, anniversaries, milestone birthdays, graduation, and buying a first home are all pivotal life moments. Celebrating collectively creates opportunities for laughter, excitement and shared moments.

92

build resilience

Believe that you can cope, connect with people or services to support you, share what you are experiencing, help others, activate positive thoughts and seek meaning. Embodying these behaviours, thoughts and actions to build personal resilience.

93

gift your presence

Notice the little things. Accept people as they are in that moment. Put down digital devices. Listen with your whole body, listen to what is in between what is being said. Sing a song. Take a stroll side by side. Create rituals and traditions.

94

relax

By taking time each day to unwind and relax, you can better manage stress, maintain balance, and enhance your quality of life. Consistent relaxation helps you recharge, enabling you to face daily challenges with a calm and centred mind.

95

enjoy the ride

Happiness isn't something you find; it's something you create along the journey of life. It's like the road trip itself, full of twists, turns, and unexpected stops. It's in the laughter of friends, the warmth of sunshine on your face, and even the quiet moments of reflection.

There is no way to happiness.
Happiness is the way.

WAYNE W. DYER

96

ground yourself

Take off your shoes, dig your toes into sand, grass or mud, and feel the sensation of the earth making contact with the skin of your feet. Close your eyes, feel the breeze or the sun or the rain on your face. Breathe deeply.

97

open your eyes

Life is like a treasure hunt for miracles, little sparks of magic hiding in plain sight. Sometimes they're as subtle as a smile from a stranger or a butterfly landing on your shoulder. But if you keep your eyes peeled, you'll find them everywhere, turning ordinary moments into extraordinary ones.

98

seek silver linings

When going through a difficult time, seek out the positives, such as lessons learned or unresolved issues that have finally surfaced. Embracing the silver linings allows you to find hope and meaning. It is a great way to foster an optimistic outlook.

99

appreciate beauty

Beauty is a product of your perception. It is the way your mind process and interpret the things you see that give them their aesthetic qualities. Beauty lies before you in the everyday ordinary. Looking at lovely things can elevate the quality of your life.

100

praise the day

Arrange a bowl of flowers, make a coffee, write a poem or say a prayer in the morning sun. Ground yourself, find serenity, and bring peace to your day with these small acts of beauty and reflection.

101

consider future you

The choices you make today lay the foundation for who you will become tomorrow. While your past experiences may have influenced your journey, they do not define you. Embracing this truth allows you to release the weight of past traumas and become an authentic and happier version of yourself.

from Cecilia

Through daily rituals, words of empowerment, and affirming quotes, I hope to support and inspire you to live your dream life filled with moments of reflection, self-discovery, and love.

If you found this book helpful, please review and share it. That helps it find its way to those who need it. This would mean a lot to me. Thank you.

Connect with me:
https://thedreamlifeproject.co
📷 @dreamlifeproject_

www.ingramcontent.com/pod-product-compliance
Lightning Source LLC
Chambersburg PA
CBHW061750070526
44585CB00025B/2849